AF219621

Nirvana for the modern Era

28 Impulses from another Dimension

by Satya Murti

सत्य मूर्ति

Production and publishing:
BoD - Books on Demand, Norderstedt
ISBN: 9783756208869

Copyright © 2022

Satya Murti

Saint Augustine

Germany

Welcome

First let me congratulate you for purchasing this little book. What you are holding in your hands seems simple but the impact could change your life forever.

Most spiritual books cover the topic of reaching the state of Nirvana, especially through the use of meditative techniques. These books are very insightful and deeply interesting but on the other hand also quite thick, extensive and demanding in terms of temporal devotion from the reader.

These days, time has become a rare good in industrialized countries, limited to 24 hours a day each individual needs proper allocation skills. Even though spiritual concepts are highly requested, long term engagement becomes impossible given the massive amount of time needed.

This book solves these problems. Without the tiniest additional cost of time each technique can easily be integrated into daily life. It remains your choice which or how many techniques to choose and when to apply them. However your selection may look like, the experiences will provide unknown dimensions for all of you.

Aligned with the daily challenges of the working individual in the 20th century these techniques fit the modern era. Even though each and every technique can indeed guide you towards the Nirvana, the primary objective is to provide insight into yet unknown interrelationships. This makes you more susceptible for spiritual influences and the more receptive you are, the deeper your spiritual experiences will be.

Way more techniques exist out there but I focused on the farthest reaching ones. Executed regularly they offer an extremely wide spectrum of experiences at maximum simplicity. Do not underestimate their potential as their subtle look, their effortless feasibility and their supposedly easy to guess impact seem harmless to the untrained eye, but the truth is, all these characteristics are actually signs of extraordinary quality, signs for the most powerful methods ever created.

Life is in every breath, death is within the same breath, you will not die on a distant day, sometime away, you are dying in this moment, you live and you die right now, simultaneously, the same way an originally empty barrel is empty and full at the same time when it gets filled with water consistently. Once aware of this you will stop suffering in the present for an imaginary, future moment of all-embracing wish-fulfilment.

Nirvana?

Nirvana stands for complete extermination. It represents a form of salvation and is a result of a sudden enlightenment, a result of an experience impossible to be captured by the mind itself. Eventually it originates from a state of conscious no-mind even.

Nirvana is not a type of growth, it is rather a form of compression and simplification, its source is an inner cleansing and a repulsion of excessive components. It all sounds vague and unprecise but this is just a matter of fact. Words come from the mind and therefore they are quite an insufficient substitute for experience. When it comes to the spiritual world special techniques convey the best experience hence the best answers. The mind might be helpful by analyzing and organizing these experiences but it cannot gain those on its own.

As a consumer you get taught that more of something cannot be bad, that growth and technological change have all the solutions for any of your problems in store so that eventually you will be blessed with almighty happiness in a nearby future, just a little bit more, just a little bit better and it will pop up. Is that the case? Has anyone of you already received that package, or do you know anybody who did?

The human species seems to be more interested in having than in being, being the only ones on planet earth having this attitude. How their lives look seems more important than how it feels. Ever since this has led to inner turmoil which even nowadays all of you can sense. So it is not without reason that from the very first day people were searching for inner peace, not for a condition characterized by hope, desire and ambition but rather by an entire absence of inner conflict.

This condition is the Nirvana. You cannot find it, you cannot search for it, but it will rather find you and overwhelm you suddenly once you are all set. This precious book will help you open up for it.

Embrace the techniques

At first glance the techniques presented in this book look quite banal. They are not supposed to challenge but to invite you. Enjoying them is the best way to stay motivated, interested and committed, and laughing about yourselves sometimes proves that you don't take things too seriously.

Eventually each and every technique represents a technique of meditation, even though they definitely do not provoke that impression at first sight.

However, meditation consists of only two fundamental components, namely the absence of thoughts and conscious awareness. The techniques build a bridge to an easier transition between daily life and meditation by making the above mentioned components possible in a playful manner, as they are otherwise both exercise-intense and difficult to master.

Probably you will start speculating about the techniques' effects and possible outcomes. Do not try to approach them with your brain, as they are not meant for the mind. Do not agonize over it, just go ahead and do it. In fact the brain is even unable to capture the impact of the techniques. Instead devote yourselves as good as you can and watch your inner processes carefully.

This self-observation is the core, the essence of the techniques. The results always represent your own experiences, there is no right or wrong, there is just realization, and its quality depends mainly on the degree of trust you put into those techniques, your openness towards new things and especially your level of devotion.

Each technique's quality is unprecedented. On the other hand its effects always depend on the individual. It is very easy to prejudge, however this is giving insight towards your attitude rather than providing clues about the quality of the techniques themselves. Are you truly looking for a change, for a new dimension of life itself? Or are you rejecting every unknown impulse just to continue your way, simply to justify your life decisions so you can feel a little better for a little while? In case you are indeed craving for something new, be aware that without a decisive change of view and behavior it won't materialize.

Rejecting disruptive ideas is actually one of the easiest ways to deal with them as there is nothing more comfortable than not even having to cope with new concepts at all. Ask yourselves whether your previous behavior has led to the results you were always hoping for, prior to being misled by premature conclusions.

Prejudging has no impact on the convict itself but it allows you to not concern yourselves with an unknown topic at all. Once confronted with objects that threaten your self-perception or worldview, a typical self-defense mechanism kicks in, called cognitive dissonance. It means negating even obvious and proven facts, especially own experiences, for the fear of the destruction of somebodies own convictions, so be aware of it at all times.

Do not view your insights, gained by grappling with the techniques, as a possible evaporation of your world, but rather as a next step, as a new level of evolution, as a sequel of your individual story. Nothing that can be destroyed did ever exist in the first place!

The reason for me to give you that speech is that you define yourselves as your mind, you rely on it solely. Without even knowing you worship your brain turning it into a saint. This is understandable in a world reigned by quantify- and provability. The mind itself does not cause the problem, but your identification does, as you really believe you have control over your mind.

The bitter truth is, you are being controlled by your mind. Your mind is very cunning and a master of deception. It was able to advance from a simple tool to an almighty ruler. You do not believe that? All right, try to shut it down. Try not to think. If you are capable of cutting out every thought for ten minutes straight, then you do not need this book, then I have to congratulate you for mastering your brain!

What to focus on

You live your life on auto-pilot. You only believe that your decisions are made consciously, in fact they are just a result of conditioning processes meanwhile internalized to full automatism, even the act of feeling is happening the way you are being taught. Only once you are aware of that mechanics you will gather a real opportunity to make a decision on your own, a true, conscious decision.

The techniques presented here offer a unique opportunity to break those mechanisms and to see through them. Executing on these techniques is not difficult at all, but the focus does not lie on the mere execution, this is just a means to an end. The real challenge is the observation of your inner processes, and that at any given time. Just watch, emphasize and collect information, do not judge, just collect. Insight will be a sheer conclusion of this process. At the end of the observation phase you can try to organize your experiences, going through important realizations once again.

The techniques are not necessarily rigid. Adjust them to your liking if another variant proofs to deliver better results. The sequence in which they are presented is random as well and does not follow any specific logic. As the techniques focus on different aspects the opportunity of combining them offers a huge variety when it comes to integrating them into your specific routines. Once you found one or more promising methods stay with them for at least four weeks, do not switch, even though they feel squeezed out, as your experiences will change over the course of time.

Never focus primarily on the technique, but completely on yourselves. Always be aware of what happens inside of you, become totally conscious at any given moment and make yourselves the center of all attention. The more things you can observe the wider the radius of your sense of self, the more comprehensive your treasure trove of experience will become. There is no target, no goal when it comes to using the techniques, time does not matter. There is no particular insight do be gained from one particular technique. All experience is highly individual, it is meant solely for you, no trophy or any type of fame awaits and for sure nobody will be interested or even impressed by the results you come up with.

What I am telling you now is extremely important; the intervals between the single moments of perception of your ever changing sensations are moments of „no-mind", moments without thoughts, especially those need to be perceived consciously.

Maybe you have seen how the Icelandic football team swears in their fans prior to every game. Everyone claps their hands to a ferocious battle cry, a few seconds pass before they clap and yell again. As the ritual continues the intervals shorten until they evaporate completely which also signals the end of the ritual. This indeed is a meditative technique. The interesting thing is that the moment of the battle cry, the element of noise, is secondary as the focus is rather being put on the conscious awareness of the intervals in between those battle cries, because those intervals are free from thought.

The process you will go through is not characterized by growth, but by death, loss and compression, the technique functions just as a means to an end. In order to achieve the best results, paradoxical intervention is used, creating a confusing scenario and therefore triggering unforeseen physiological and mental reactions. Consciously observing those reactions will eventually build the foundation for any spiritual transformation.

I am totally aware that reduction and loss are no big incentives for you at all, but let me tell you this, during Buddha's lifetime he was not about to be worshiped, he was rather avoided and banned exactly for that reason. His teachings were so far from the norm, so contrary to common beliefs that he was always recognized as a threat, as a troublemaker, an intruder. People simply got scared by his convictions and even though this has changed over the centuries and lots of people are now following his doctrine, you still block other dimensions out of your life. Be brave, take your convictions to the test; if they can be destroyed by the truth, they deserve to be destroyed by the truth. Always remember that within destruction there is creation at the same time as well.

28 Impulses

from another Dimension

1.

Enter the longest queue

Whether you are at the supermarket, the post office or at the town hall, it does not matter, always look for the longest queue. Instead of going for a quick in and out, I ask you to intentionally do the complete opposite.

Make it a conscious decision. The more you are in a hurry the more effective this technique will be. Control your inner frenzy, stay completely calm, take a look around and observe the people. Take a closer look at the room itself, stare into the emptiness, close your eyes and find the silence hidden inside of you.

Your mind will declare you crazy, but this is the only way to take back control over it. You can make the decision that time does not matter at that particular moment, just because you consciously say so. But not only this, further more you can even enjoy this short oasis of peace.

Watch the stress around you and realize on the contrary your own physiological stillness, this way even your mind calms down. Become aware of the control you can exercise and see how tiny the consequences of some wasted minutes are. Instead of ongoing silent complaints due to the long wait, you were even able to bestow some peace to yourselves simply by consciously experiencing these few minutes.

2.

Name a spider

In every house there is at least one small spider to find. Usually most of you will tend to eliminate that kind of bugs. Some of you might find them disgusting or even scary.

Choose a spider that has in some way a distinct look, one that can easily be recognized among others and give it a name. This name can be a funny or an exotic one, simply avoid names without you having any association connected to it.

Whenever you see that spider, treat it like a dog or a cat, simply like a pet. Talk to it, ask questions and let it become a part of your world, similar to a roommate. Tell it good night and greet it in the morning. Just try it and see what effects that behavior has on you.

3.

While writing an email, stop abruptly and stare at a random corner of your screen for at least 30 seconds

Those who work a lot on PC will prefer this technique as it is easy and regularly implementable. It is very important to execute it at a random situation. At an unpredictable moment, simply stop typing, in the middle of a sentence, in the middle of a word.

The moment you recall this technique is probably the best time to go for it and stop typing. Do not think for long, just do it, freeze in your current position and stare at a corner of your screen. Make sure you do not watch the corner precisely, but rather see through it so it turns blurry.

During execution, empty your mind, from one moment to the next just stop thinking. All you do is stare and breath. Do not allow any thought to enter your world. In case thoughts do pop up, focus consciously on the chosen corner of the screen, scanning it for every little detail, for its material, its graining and for its slightest variation of color.

4.

Pretend to be hoarse and avoid talking consequently

Look for a situation in which not-talking is a minor issue. You should probably avoid an important business meeting, but a get-together with friends seems suitable.

Consciously refuse to talk to anyone at all. In case somebody points out your silence try to pretend being hoarse as authentically as possible even though it is only pantomimic.

It is important to choose a situation where you would normally be quite talkative. Do not try to communicate by gestures or other means either. Do not intervene any conversation, only listen. The longer you are able to follow through the more intense the experience will be.

Compare the new situation with the traditional one, what is different, what does it feel like? Is it easy or difficult for you, do you feel burdened or freed, does it probably even make you go crazy? For sure this situation will be unfamiliar at the least, but this is what the technique is supposed to induce.

5.

When you go to bed, lay down on your back and put one hand flat on your belly

At nights, shortly before falling asleep, we tend to be the most tranquil. This situation is suited best for numerous techniques as you are conscious enough to observe while at the same time there is absence of activity which would normally interfere during daytime.

Once you put one hand, and only one, flat on your belly, either on a thin shirt or straight on your skin, you will experience pleasant warmth spreading from your stomach within seconds.

Focus completely on this warmth, follow it. Let it travel throughout your entire body. Observe what it does to you. Instead of using your hand, you can also take a small and light pillow as a substitute, especially if you want to make that technique a habit.

Leave all thoughts aside, rather concentrate on all body parts that are being conquered by the warmth. At times you could even try to navigate that warmth yourselves using your own will. Do not try to stay awake at all cost, falling asleep is okay. Should you suffer from sleeping issues this technique can probably even help with this.

At any time, put one hand to your heart, close your eyes and feel your heartbeat

Touching your body while mentally focused enhances the connection. When bodybuilders face problems accessing certain muscle groups, touching the equivalent region helps the central nervous system to strengthen the interaction between the brain and the appropriate muscle.

You will get the best results when you choose a situation in which you can suddenly stop your action, or even the better you instantly use the technique once you observe an upcoming emotion, best suited are anger or fear.

Always be self-aware in these situations, watch what happens to the upcoming feeling, does it leave? Is that something that you are capable of watching at all, can you probably even gain control over your emotion or is it rather being enhanced?

The heartbeat is one of the most calming sounds of all. If you keep practicing for a while you will be able to feel your heartbeat at any given time, even without physical contact.

7.

When you listen to music, let it flow through your entire body

This technique sounds way easier than it truly is. Remember the times when you heard music without understanding the words. Each word is just a sound in itself, without significance. It is only through the understanding of language that a word becomes more than just a sound, it carries a meaning, and this meaning is the reason why you are listening to music with your brain nowadays.

It is very difficult to perceive a word without automatically associating a meaning or an image to it. This is why songs without lyrics suit better in the beginning but on the other hand the closer you are to a song the more intense the revelations will be.

If possible go outdoors, use earphones, close your eyes, bow your head, turn up the volume and focus on absolutely nothing, just let go. Let the music flow through your body, only the sounds. Imagine yourselves as a wire overwhelmed with electricity, there is no interpretation, no understanding. You simply turn into a vessel being filled up with notes.

Should you indeed be able to accomplish that, the experience will be outstanding. The more you let go, the further away your mind, the better it will work out.

When you go for a walk, focus on one aspect only

When you go out for a walk everything else attracts your attention except the walk itself. Do not lose heart if this technique freaks you out at first as your mind will continuously travel around, everything needs its time.

When you focus on something it should have to do with yourselves. You could observe your breathing or the movement of your arms. You could even try to feel the wind blowing through your hair or caressing your face, the sound of your footsteps is also a viable option, actually there is no limit of what to observe.

No matter what you choose, stick to it for the whole duration of the walk, do not switch around. Should your mind drift apart, and it will drift apart, focus on the chosen aspect again as soon as possible.

For sure it will be exhausting at the beginning but over time this feeling will give way for other emotions. The more vigilant you are in observing yourselves the more changes you will notice, both physically and mentally.

Choose a very special food in the supermarket

That does not sound spectacular at all, so let me explain. This food must be something you are craving for. I want you to have a very precise picture of what you are going to do with it, and this activity should turn into an event.

If it is candy for example, celebrate its consumption. Imagine a scenario of when and how you will eat it. Imagine the ambience, the whole setting. All of this must be set up in your head already, prior to the purchase. You can choose whatever you like, an extraordinary sauce, a particular piece of meat, even spices, but you have to buy it for a special, predefined moment.

The most important thing is the detailed planning of the event of consumption and its execution. Ensure you are looking forward to this particular moment and make it only yours, own it. Consider it a secret baby-reward.

Of course the event should capture most of your attention, not necessarily the purchase itself. No matter how extensive, how time consuming, no matter the amount of preparation, merge into it, celebrate it, let yourselves get absorbed by it. This is supposed to be the essence of this technique, enjoy the moment to the fullest, simply savor, not a single thought should take away your pleasure.

10.

If your mobile rings, ignore it for at least 30 minutes

At least once per day, at a time of your choice, free yourselves from the mobile-autopilot-mode. In case somebody calls or sends a text, do not check on the display but rather ignore it for at least 30 minutes.

Of course your mind will come up with reasons why you urgently have to check the mobile instantly, but none of these reasons truly exist. The mobile has already taken a huge chunk of freedom from you, now it is time for revenge!

For those who react almost instinctively to any signal from their mobile, this adjustment will be massive. Withstand the desire to respond once it rings, right at the time you resist that first intention, just at this particular moment, you have to start watching your emotions precisely. Scan your thoughts, turn into a witness, into a silent observer.

Do this as long as possible and put special emphasis on how thoughts and feelings change over time. Whatever happens, do not give in, as with

every day you successfully execute on this technique
you will win back a piece of autonomy.

11.

When watching TV but you cannot find something interesting, turn it off for several minutes

This won't be too difficult at all, but of course this technique is not about turning of the TV itself. Instead realize how silence kicks in from one moment to the next, within a blink of an eye.

Try to catch the moment of transition, that particular second where everything turns quiet. This is a very special instance of change, not only because raucous sounds suddenly disappear, but also a significant visual stimulus evaporates simultaneously. If you only muted the sound you would miss it.

Feel what happens inside of you, the first 30 seconds are vital. How does your body respond during the transition from noise to silence, does your body relax? Pay attention to the steady tone that appears instantly after turning off the TV and see how it evolves.

12.

When using your mind, avoid thoughts related to the past or the future

Every now and then you will be lost in thought. Once you manage to catch a moment in which you become consciously aware of the thinking process itself you should try this technique.

You can easily allow every thought but observe them accurately. In case they relate to the past or the future, resolve them instantly, stop thinking at once. In the beginning trying this for 10 minutes is sufficient as it will be very exhausting for sure.

You will gather deep insights into the quality of your thoughts. Additionally you will get a better feel for the nature of thoughts in general. Dissolving multiple processes might be frustrating at first but what you learn by doing this matters way more than anything else.

This technique provides fundamental revelations of how your brain works and in which situations thoughts are helpful and in which they are not.

13.

Softly run your fingertips over your collarbone

The skin at the collarbone is relatively thin and the closer you get to the breastbone the more sensitive it gets. This technique is perfect for redirecting your focus to the inside.

When you are watching TV and feel relaxed, softly caress your bare collarbone and upper chest area a couple of times. Execute very slowly, close your eyes and concentrate solely on the contact itself.

As usual self-observation is the Holy Grail. How do you feel after some time? A touch is vital for human beings and can have multiple effects on the individual. Touching yourselves is usually not as intense as another person's touch, but surprisingly the effects differ when it comes to the area around the collarbone.

14.

Do not ask people what they have done yesterday or what they are about to do tomorrow

Empirically those questions are standard, especially among couples. Do not intend to ask such questions for an entire day.

Particularly in partnerships silence becomes an important aspect, constant conversations tend to go in circles and distract you from seizing the moment. Once you consciously try to avoid the mentioned phrases you will be surprised most likely by how often you are actually about to use them.

This technique is not about communicating differently. Its goal is not, to fade out neither the past nor the future. Observing the consequences for your inner world when being forced to avoid those themes is what it is all about. You will be thrown back to your center once you have to stop talking abruptly for the reason of not being allowed to say what you intended to.

If you are able to put yourselves into question, this technique could turn into a fantastic experience.

Maybe you will start laughing about yourselves when even for the tenth time in a row you are unable to begin a conversation. You will probably realize the importance of activity and engagement in your life and you will also get a first glimpse of your thoughts' content.

15.

Instead of looking for reasons why something cannot be done, find options to make it happen and execute on it

The prime example is sports, of course. It is utterly fascinating how many reasons you come up with of why things cannot be done, even though you assure your absolute will to implement them if there only was enough time.

Was there ever such a thing connected to your job? Of course not, as your job inhabits the ultimate first place on your priority list, with a massive lead, but surprisingly you would never admit that. This is not a judgement at all, it is simply a fact.

A job is not optional in your opinion, everything else is. Your whole life is being organized around it. There is never a reason for not going to work. It would never cross your mind to explain to your boss one day later why you simply did not show up yesterday. You always manage to jiggle things around so that nothing collides with your working hours.

The reason why all this runs so smoothly is your attitude. So this attitude is what I am asking you to transfer onto other projects. Find a way to do things which you supposedly never had time for and stick to it at all cost, the same way you do it with a job!

16.

If something you really crave for catches your eye, and you could get it right at that point, hold on nevertheless

Consumption is the fundamental concept in industrialized countries. It is inseparably connected to a wish, to a desire. Without even noticing it any more you are being bombarded non-stop with all kind of advertisement, a tool carefully designed to provoke that desire.

This technique is precious in multiple ways as it both shows you the nature of desire in general and provides you with the insight of what happens to it once it is left unsatisfied.

Should you accidentally face an object of desire, whatever it may be, do not give in, resist for at least two days. Observe yourselves closely, how do you feel within the first minutes, how does this feeling change over the course of the day and what happens to your thoughts?

The deeper your self-observation, the more intense, the broader the resulting experience will be, the greater the comprehension will become.

17.

When in a room with several people, whatever happens, do not use your mobile

Using the mobile has become an unconscious habit these days. Without further thought you look at it at all times, automatically.

When you find yourselves among other people you are familiar with, watch carefully what happens once one of them pulls out their mobile. What happens to the group, what effect does that have on you as well as on the atmosphere in the room?

Avoid using your mobile consciously, how does that feel? How do group dynamics change? Do the mobiles vanish after a while or do the conversations instead, how does the situation proceed?

Be prepared to merely act as an observing witness whilst in the room. Do not influence the situation, simply stay aware of what is going on and of its impact on yourselves and on your emotional state, do you feel lonely, comfortable or sad maybe?

At any time you have the chance to impact your life, to involve things, to remove things. Nothing just happens automatically, you are making decisions more often than you think, but you are simply not making them consciously.

18.

Spend an entire day without watching the clock

When it comes to industrialized countries, time has turned into an extremely rare good and in most cases the clock takes over the part of the whip. Everyone possesses an inner clock though and once you are able to turn away from any physical watch for longer, you will realize your ability to develop a pretty precise feeling for the actual time of day.

This technique is difficult to put into practice. There are clocks everywhere, they are waiting for you around every corner, even the cover of your mobile is equipped with it and calendars have already become a part of everyday life the same way breathing has.

Of course this technique is primarily about observing the consequences for your inner world. How difficult is it to execute on it, what does that reveal to you, how does it make you feel? Obviously all of this sounds pretty therapeutic, but it is not supposed to.

Any sort of healing or behavior modification is not the major concern here. It is all about experiencing, about revealing things that were formerly unknown or only a part of philosophical considerations. Value-free experience is fundamental for all forms of wisdom as without it understanding would become impossible and the more unconventional that experience is the more valuable its results.

19.

Feel an object

Indeed every object is suitable for this technique, consciously feel it, take your time, close your eyes and try to discover everything the object has to offer. As you can use whatever you like, this technique can be executed anytime and anyplace. Especially fluffy objects are worthwhile being swept through your face even. Generally speaking the more complex the object is, in a haptic sense, the better.

It is vital to take yourselves out of a given situation purposely, interrupt every current action and focus solely on touching. Everything about the object becomes relevant, its shape, its temperature, its texture and every single detail, as tiny as it may be. The more you are involved in something that you could possibly stop doing the more intense the experience will be, therefore this technique works best at the job.

The center of your attention is not supposed to belong to the object alone, do not forget to observe yourselves in order to witness the changes of your emotional state. Interrupting your daily routine in such a manner regularly will provide increasing insight.

20.

While the sun is shining, close your eyes and feel the sunrays on your face

Most techniques are built to draw you out of the autopilot-mode, this one here as well. Stop whatever you are currently doing, close your eyes and turn your face towards the sun.

While doing this, focus completely on your face, simply relax and feel how your skin reacts to the sunlight, devote yourselves totally to this warmth, become a vessel for it. Observe what is both happening to your body and your mind.

Stay like this for at least two minutes. Even though that does not sound like a long period, with your eyes closed and fully focused on just one thing, two minutes can easily feel like two hours.

Stay consciously aware during the whole process, let everything else disappear, the noise, the thoughts. Devotion has become very rare in an environment where the concept of control and independence is so dominant. View the sun as a superior object, open up to it completely and let its sunrays dive deep inside of you until they spill over.

21.

Do not judge

Each language only exists due to the duality of the mind. There is no cold without warm, no wrong without right. You are judging constantly, whether it is through thoughts, words or actions. You will only become fully aware of this fact once this technique is consequently utilized.

Make sure that for an entire day you are not judging while talking or thinking. Whatever you do, ask yourselves whether there might still be some baby-judgement left, secretly hidden somewhere.

It is absolutely natural to have preferences and aversions. Even though perceiving something as good or bad is indeed a judgement, you should rather focus primarily on avoiding categorical valuations. Recognize the underlying morals and be amoral yourselves, meaning neither moral nor unmoral at all, let facts speak!

Simply give it a try and do not forget to register your emotions along the way. Realize what happens to your thoughts and how often you indeed do judge. Ask yourselves whether you have been consciously aware of it.

22.

At nights, stand on a patio and stare at the moon

At nights the silence is almost tangible. Just go outdoors when all is dark, the less lights the better. Stare at the moon and feel the cold.

Put special emphasis on that particular first moment you enter open skies. At nights fragrances seem more intense but only for a limited time, until your nose gets used to it. Therefore focus solely on the fragrance at first.

Just stay outside, watch the moon and enjoy the moment. Pay attention to the stillness, the cold. Realize how the nature of objects is being transformed by the darkness, how different all sounds feel.

Remain without thought for a few minutes, simply aware of all impressions the night has to offer, what impact does that have on you?

23.

Among friends, only do listen

The consequences of silence for your entire organism are massively underestimated. While the other person is still speaking, you are already thinking about an answer. This technique is not about proper listening, but rather about silence, not only about silence in terms of acoustics, but primarily about the silence of the mind.

Lots of things will change once your intention switches from rapid answering to patient smiling instead. Do not teach or correct anyone, do not even check the truthfulness of what is being said, just smile and remain silent. Obviously you should answer upcoming questions, but each answer should redirect the flow of the conversation back to somebody else without you making a significant statement.

That will be a true challenge for most, as you are all so eager to spread your opinion. Once you are able to abstain from doing exactly this, the results for your inner world will be astonishing.

Multiple times per day, watch your posture

Taking a look at the outside is an easy thing to do as it simply requires the opening of your eyes. Looking inside on the other hand only happens in case of emergency, only when the first impulse comes from your body, namely by contacting you through pain.

Looking inside is not only improving the quality of life significantly, it also provides great insight into other dimensions of your being the more skilled you become.

At any time, just take a moment to inspect each detail of your current posture, whether you are sitting or standing, without using a mirror, but simply by empathizing with your inner self. What is the position of your head, how are your shoulders positioned? Which leg carries more weight and what about the rotation of your pelvis?

As you see, it is impossible to fall short of potential regions to inspect. Repeat that regularly but always remember that the most important question remains the same: Through self-observation, how does the technique affect you?

25.

During work, breath in and out deeply, at least ten times

An all-time classic, but even though the effectiveness of such a simple technique is widely known, it is regularly being ignored for its ordinary and unsophisticated look.

As usual the details make the difference. First you should consciously step aside from your current activity. The breathing should not happen automatically, instinctively, it needs to be celebrated instead, worshiped even. Empty your mind and prepare devotedly for a conscious experience of an otherwise unconscious process.

Close your eyes and follow every breath, feel your ribcage extending and your belly widening. Feel the temperature of the breath in your nose and in your throat. Follow it throughout your body and let it travel long distance. Breath as deeply as possible, both in, but particularly out, breath out until all air has vanished completely. The transition between gasps has its own beauty, observe yourselves closely during these moments, recognize those breaks as discrete elements.

There are multiple available aspects to watch, even though we are talking about such a basic action like breathing. It is on you to squeeze the most out of this technique as complexity is not necessarily a reflection of ingenuity.

26.

Contemplate a flower in open nature

The area around you is crowded with lifeless and artificially created material. No matter where you look, roads, cars, parking areas, buildings and even play areas, almost everything you are surrounded by is the absence of nature.

Finding a flower that you can smell without picking it up is not as easy as you might think. Try it whenever you are outdoors. At first inspect it very carefully, watch every detail, especially the petal with its very unique haptics is a sight to see, recognize its overall beauty, its simplicity.

Try to touch and feel the flower without damaging it. Smell it, literally suck up its fragrance. Recognize its character, everything it consists of, what do you like most about it? Take as much time as you wish, even though it ends up to be a short rendezvous only.

Each and every one of you is a natural object, organically grown, full of energy, which is why every contact with other organically grown objects is substantially different to those who are artificially created.

27.

Leave your mobile at home

Without thought you automatically catch your mobile while leaving the house. It is no longer a conscious decision anymore, it just happens. But what would take place if you left it alone? I do not want a sophisticated answer but I rather want you to experience it!

Try the experiment, including an evaluation. You can start small by using only short time periods first, but be honest when it comes to analyzing the consequences. What repercussions occur, have you been limited in your scope of action? Was it important to react to certain things immediately?

Way more important however is the question of what that missing mobile provoked. Were you probably nervous or even terrified? Did you feel less stressed or on the opposite even more stressed out, or did you feel a certain kind of freedom instead?

All the answers to these questions do actually not give an idea about the importance of your mobile for your life, but they rather reveal a lot about you. All the insight that this experiment can deliver is meant to enable a closer look at yourselves, generating a feel for what you truly are. This is indeed the essence of each technique presented in this book.

28.

Look at a written text in your mother tongue without reading it

This technique is almost a stroke of genius, that effective and deep it is. Take some time for its execution as it may seem weird and impossible to do at first glance.

Search for a text, written in your mother tongue, it does not have to be a long one, but it should consist of more than just one word only. You need to be able to read every single word and you should not stay that far away from the text so that it can easily turn blurry. Billboards and ads fulfil that purpose pretty well.

You will realize very quickly that you are reading every word instantly, you do not see its shape, its structure, like a child would, instead you are reading automatically, and with this being the case each word receives a meaning, and this meaning forces a reaction inside of you without you having a chance fighting it.

Now try not to read the text. Watch it, but find a way to suppress reading it. Recognize its shape and view every written word as a symbol only, as a sequence of sub-symbols which are meaningless once isolated. If you manage to observe yourselves precisely along the way, magical things will happen.